SCIENCE Q&A

EARTH SCIENCE

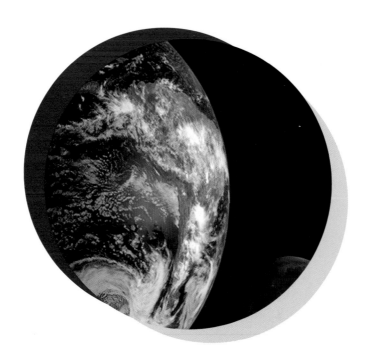

Cavendish
Square
New York

Published in 2016 by Cavendish Square Publishing, LLC
243 5th Avenue, Suite 136, New York, NY 10016

First Edition

Website: cavendishsq.com

CPSIA Compliance Information: Batch #WS15CSQ

Library of Congress Cataloging-in-Publication Data

Earth science / edited by Tim Harris.
p. cm. — (Science Q&A)
Includes index.
ISBN 978-1-50260-616-7 (hardcover) ISBN 978-1-50260-615-0 (paperback)
ISBN 978-1-50260-617-4 (ebook)
1. Earth sciences — Juvenile literature. I. Harris, Tim. II. Title.

QE29.H37 2015
550—d23

For Brown Bear Books Ltd:
Editors: Tracey Kelly, Dawn Titmus, Tim Harris
Designer: Mary Walsh
Design Manager: Keith Davis
Editorial Director: Lindsey Lowe
Children's Publisher: Anne O'Daly
Picture Manager: Sophie Mortimer

Picture Credits:
T=Top, C=Center, B=Bottom, L=Left, R=Right

Front Cover : All pictures NASA GRIN/NIX.
Inside: NASA: APOD/NOAO/AURA/NSF 6tr, Apollo Gallery 18r, 19t, 19b, 21tr, ESA 26cl, GRIN 26b, JPL, 5tl, 14tl, 15cr; Mt Palomar Observatory 9r, NIX 4, 5br, 6-7, 8cl, 9l, 10tl, 14b, 18tl, 23tr, 23b, 26tl, 27; Shutterstock: 11b, Benintende 11t, Marcel Clemens 7tr, Byron W Moore 15t, Jurgen Ziewe 10tr; Thinkstock: FAE 22bl, Hemera 22tl, iStockphoto 1, 6t, Photos.com 22r

Brown Bear Books has made every attempt to contact the copyright holder.
If you have any information please contact licensing@brownbearbooks.co.uk

Printed in the United States of America

CONTENTS

—INTRODUCTION—

With its spectacular landscapes and specialized habitats, Earth is home to a rich variety of animals, plants—and humans. Natural processes acting on Earth make life possible.

Earth is the only planet in our solar system on which organisms—plants, animals, and people—are able to live. It is a fascinating world of extremes, with natural forces at work above and below the surface. A complex water system called the hydrosphere and finely tuned habitats such as rain forests support life for the many species of plants and animals that live here. Have you ever looked at a landscape—a desert, forest, or mountain range—and wondered how it was created? Or have you thought about why we have four seasons—spring, summer, winter, and fall—or what makes the climate vary in different parts of the world and how this affects the whole world's environment?

◀ High winds can top 155 mph (250 kmh) near the center of a hurricane, demolishing everything in its path.

◄ A herd of elephants lives in a habitat that is balanced perfectly for its particular needs for water and food.

In this book, you will learn all about how the continents were formed and how the oceans, rivers, and streams continue to sculpt the landscape. You will discover the molten metals bubbling deep within the core of Earth, and the wealth of minerals contained in the crust, from granite and marble to pyrite and flint. You will learn about nature's dramatic events, from volcanoes—vents in mountains that throw out boiling hot rock and ash—to tornados, hurricanes, and tsunamis, which sometimes flatten everything in their paths.

In the twenty-first century, changes to Earth's atmosphere and environment made by people have put some habitats at risk. But by conserving energy and finding ways to curb deforestation, we can help keep Earth a healthy place to live.

► Rocky cliffs jut out from the Rio Grande Gorge in New Mexico, where the river flows along a rift valley.

PLANET EARTH

Earth is the only planet in the solar system that supports life. It takes just over 365 days to make one complete orbit of the sun. Earth spins on its axis every twenty-four hours.

Earth's axis is tilted at 23 degrees, and this tilt gives our planet its seasons. Earth has a core at the center, a solid mantle, and a thin crust. Its chemical makeup is mostly iron, oxygen, silicon, and magnesium. The core is mostly iron and is very hot—the temperature in the inner core is probably about 9,806° Fahrenheit (5,430° Celsius).

KEY FACTS

Age: 4.5 billion years

Radius at equator: 3,967 miles (6,384 km)

Radius at poles: 3,948 miles (6,353 km)

Speed of orbit around sun: 67,108 mph (108,000 kmh)

Earth's outer shell is made of individual plates, called tectonic plates. These are made from the crust and the topmost part of the mantle. As the mantle material slowly moves, so do the plates. When two plates move apart, molten rock rises from below, filling the gap. The continents are stuck on the plates, so as the plates move, the continents move with them. Volcanic activity, earthquakes, and mountain building all happen when two plates come together.

Above the Surface

Much of the surface of Earth (71 percent) is covered by water—in the oceans, freshwater lakes, and frozen polar regions. Together, these are described as the hydrosphere. The Earth has a well-developed atmosphere, composed mostly of nitrogen (78 percent) and oxygen

HIGHEST AND LOWEST

The highest point on Earth's surface is Mount Everest in the Himalayan mountain chain. It rises to 29,028 feet (8,848 m) above sea level. The Himalayas formed from the collision of the Indian and Eurasian tectonic plates. The lowest point on the crust is Challenger Deep, in the Marianas Trench of the western Pacific Ocean. This trenchlike valley in the ocean floor is 33,432 feet (10,190 m) deep— deeper than Everest is tall.

▲ The Great Barrier Reef runs for 1,615 miles (2,600 km) along the northeast coast of Australia.

▲ The East Africa Rift Valley runs along the edge of the Somali and Nubian tectonic plates.

▲ Earth, showing the continents of South and North America and the Pacific and Atlantic oceans.

(21 percent). Three-quarters of the atmosphere's mass is concentrated in a layer just 7 miles (11 km) deep; it extends much higher, gradually

▼ The summit of Mount Everest is the highest point on Earth's surface.

thinning. As well as providing oxygen and water vapor for life, the atmosphere reduces harmful ultraviolet emissions from the sun, causes small meteors to burn up before they can reach the surface, and moderates temperatures.

The Seasons

For six months of the year, the Northern Hemisphere is slightly closer to the sun. For the other six months, the Southern Hemisphere is closer. Earth's tilt varies the length

of day and night and the amount of sunlight reaching different latitudes.

Earth has a strong magnetic field, whose poles are close to (but not the same as) the geographic North Pole and South Pole.

Earth has one natural satellite, the moon, which is on average 239,000 miles (384,400 km) away. The moon's gravity pulls the water in Earth's oceans to make the tides.

GENERAL INFORMATION

● Earth orbits the sun at a distance of 91–94 million miles (147–152 million km).

● Earth's crust is thickest beneath the Himalayan mountains— 47 miles (75 km). The crust under the oceans is much thinner, usually less than 6 miles (10 km).

Q ## What is inside Earth?

A The thin outer layer of Earth (below) is called the crust. Beneath this is the solid mantle that makes up most of Earth. The mantle is a mixture of rocks and minerals. Right at the center of Earth is the core of molten iron and nickel. The inner part of the core is very hot; scientists estimate its temperature reaches 9,806°F (5,430°C).

Q ## How were the continents formed?

A Scientists believe that the continents (below) were formed from one giant landmass known as Pangaea. This broke in two, then split up into smaller landmasses. These drifted apart until they reached their present places. But they are still moving.

286–248 million years ago

213–144 million years ago

65–25 million years ago

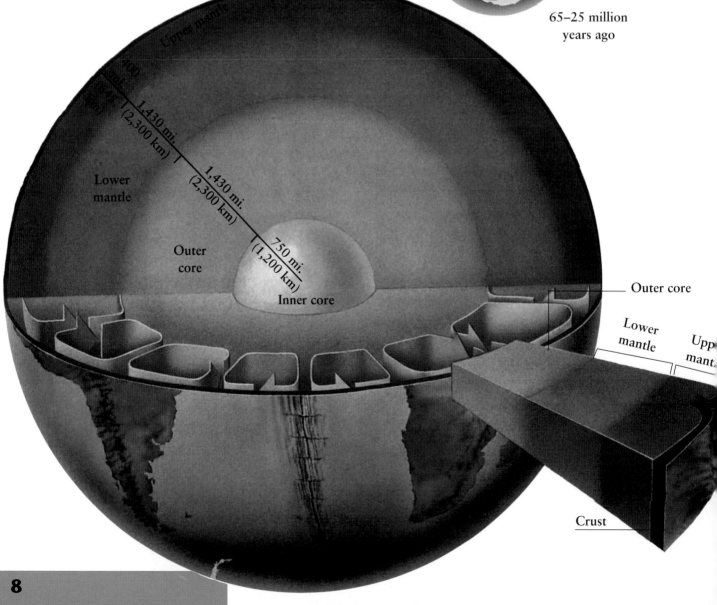

Upper mantle

1,430 mi. (2,300 km)

1,430 mi. (2,300 km)

750 mi. (1,200 km)

Lower mantle

Outer core

Inner core

Outer core

Lower mantle

Upper mantle

Crust

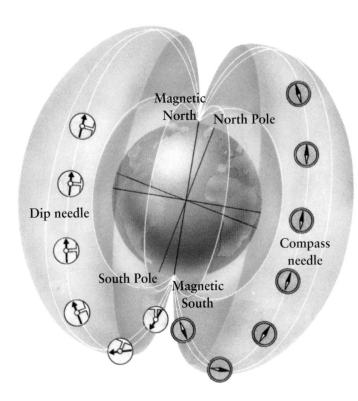

Q Why do we have seasons?

A Earth takes one year to move around the sun. But Earth is tilted on its axis. This means that different parts of Earth receive different amounts of sunlight, and so they become warmer or colder as Earth travels on its journey. When the North Pole is nearest to the sun, the northern part of Earth is warmest. Here, it is summer. At the same time, the southern part is tilted away from the sun and is cooler. Here, it is winter.

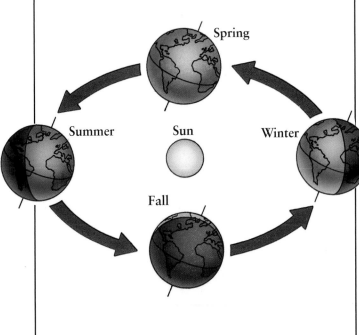

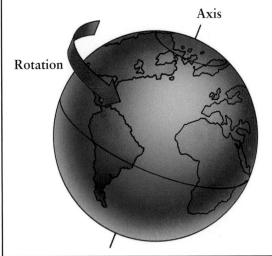

Q Why does a compass needle point north?

A Earth is like a huge magnet with a force field that covers its whole surface (above). The poles of the magnet are near the North and South Poles. Magnetized objects—such as compass needles—are drawn to these poles. Therefore, one end of a compass needle will always point north.

Q What were the ice ages?

A The ice ages (right) were periods in history when Earth became extremely cold. The last ice age ended about 10,000 years ago. Near the poles, a lot of water froze into ice. This meant that there was less water in the sea, and the sea level dropped, leaving large land areas uncovered.

Earth during ice age

Earth today

NATURAL FORCES

Powerful natural forces are acting on Earth all the time. They come from within the mantle and crust, and from the oceans and atmosphere.

KEY FACTS
Biggest volcanic eruption:
Tambora, 1815
Deadliest tsunami: Indian Ocean, 2004
Deadliest flood: China, 1931

Movements of tectonic plates and plumes of hot material in the mantle produce volcanoes and earthquakes. Volcanoes happen either where one plate is being pushed under another, causing molten rock (magma) to rise to the surface, or where plumes of hot magma rise up into Earth's crust.

Volcanic eruptions can take several forms, ranging from sheets of magma oozing relatively quietly from the opening (caldera) of the

volcano, to violent explosions of dust and bombs of red-hot rocks. When a volcano erupts, lots of gases are released, particularly sulfur

THE TAMBORA ERUPTION
The biggest volcanic eruption in recorded history was Mount Tambora, Indonesia, in 1815. The long-dormant volcano is situated over a zone where one tectonic plate is being pushed under another. The explosion was heard 1,615 miles (2,600 km) away, and the mountain lost 4,920 feet (1,500 m) in height. Thousands of people died, and the cloud of fumes spread around the world. Crops could not grow in Europe or North America in 1816, leading to the worst famine of the nineteenth century.

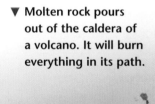

▼ Molten rock pours out of the caldera of a volcano. It will burn everything in its path.

dioxide. Eruptions often burn crops and buildings, and the explosions drop heavy debris on buildings and people, with disastrous results.

Earthquakes

When two of Earth's plates move against each other, pressure builds up along the boundary. Often the plates are locked together, unable to move as the pressure increases.

▲ Floodwater can be immensely powerful—and destructive.

▼ **This tornado looks very dark because of all the dust and debris that is twisting around in it.**

Eventually, the stress is so great that the crust tears, and the masses of rock jump past one another. Shock waves quickly spread out, shaking buildings, trees, and bridges. This is an earthquake, and it can cause great damage. Sometimes many people die as a result.

Storms and Floods

Storms are created by movements of the atmosphere. The biggest storms are called hurricanes and cyclones. The winds in some of these storms are strong enough to blow down trees and lift the roofs off buildings. Storms can whip the ocean surface into destructive waves that may damage shipping and buildings along the coast. Massive electrical charges build up in some storm clouds, which produce lightning and thunder.

A tornado, or twister, is like a small hurricane in that strong winds are sucked into a kind of tube of low pressure. A tornado may be only several feet across, but its winds may reach 250 mph (400 kmh).

GENERAL INFORMATION

● Wind speeds are measured using the Beaufort scale. Force 1 on the scale is a light air, and force 12 is a destructive hurricane.

● One of the worst months ever for tornadoes was April 2011. More than three hundred struck the southern United States, killing 359 people.

▲ **In 2005, Hurricane Katrina swirls toward New Orleans, Louisiana.**

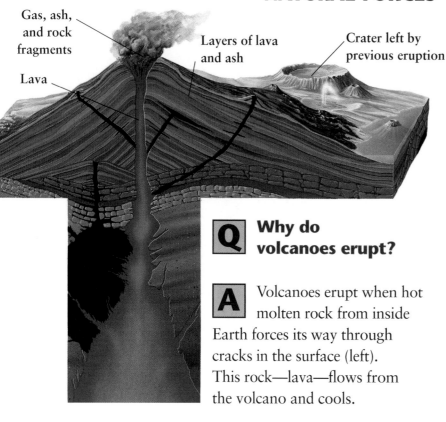

Gas, ash, and rock fragments

Layers of lava and ash

Crater left by previous eruption

Lava

Q What is a hurricane?

A A hurricane is a very strong whirling storm (right). The winds near the center can top 155 mph (250 kmh). Hurricanes begin over warm tropical seas. The surface water heats up and evaporates to form clouds. This releases the heat and makes the clouds rise. Air is sucked in from the surrounding area, swirling the clouds into a spiral. At the very center of the hurricane is a calm area called the eye. As hurricanes move, they push the sea into huge waves and may cause floods. When the hurricane reaches land, it slowly grows weaker. But the high winds can still cause great damage to buildings and trees.

Q Why do volcanoes erupt?

A Volcanoes erupt when hot molten rock from inside Earth forces its way through cracks in the surface (left). This rock—lava—flows from the volcano and cools.

Q What is a seismograph?

A A seismograph measures earthquakes. When an earthquake occurs, its hanging arm shakes, and the pen marks the paper on the revolving drum.

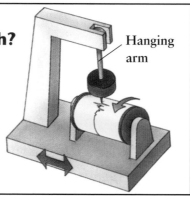

Hanging arm

Q How do we measure wind speed?

A The speed of the wind is measured on the Beaufort scale. This goes from 0 (calm) to 12 (hurricane). The scale describes how things behave at different wind speeds (right). At 1, light air and smoke drifts slowly. At force 6, large trees sway, and at force 10, buildings may be damaged.

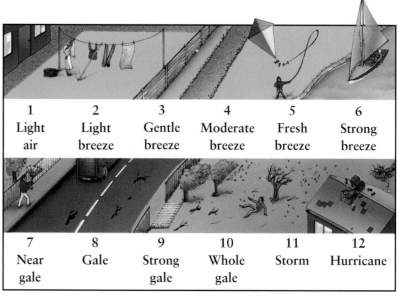

1 Light air	2 Light breeze	3 Gentle breeze	4 Moderate breeze	5 Fresh breeze	6 Strong breeze
7 Near gale	8 Gale	9 Strong gale	10 Whole gale	11 Storm	12 Hurricane

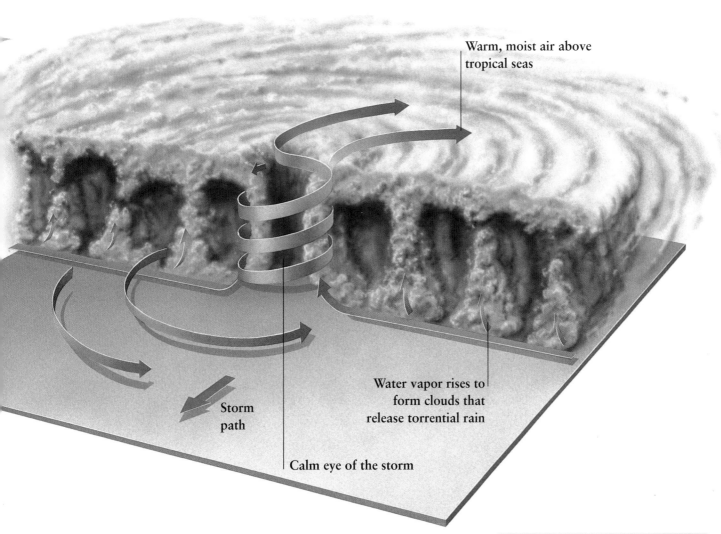

Warm, moist air above tropical seas

Water vapor rises to form clouds that release torrential rain

Storm path

Calm eye of the storm

Q Where does the wind come from?

A When air becomes warm, it rises. Cool air is sucked in to replace it, and this movement of air causes a wind. The warm air expands and cools before falling to the land again. This constant movement of air forms a regular pattern of winds around the world (right).

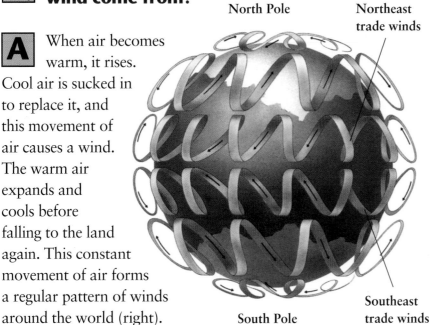

North Pole

Northeast trade winds

Southeast trade winds

South Pole

Q What causes lightning?

A Lightning is caused when a large electric charge builds up in a cloud, as a result of ice and water particles rubbing together. The electric charge flashes to Earth, or to another cloud, as lightning (above).

13

WATER

Water is found in the oceans, freshwater lakes, glaciers and ice caps, and groundwater. There is also water in the atmosphere and in plants and animals. All this water forms the hydrosphere.

KEY FACTS

Salt water: 97.5 percent
Freshwater: 2.5 percent
Frozen: 1.7 percent
Liquid: 98.3 percent

Without water, life on Earth could not survive. People and animals need clean water to drink, and so do plants. In some parts of the world, this is not always possible, and up to five million people die every year because their water is polluted or carries diseases.

Crops need rain or irrigation water. There is hardly a branch of industry that does not depend on a reliable supply of water. Water drives the turbines of hydroelectric power plants and cools the reactors in nuclear power plants that make the electricity we need.

The Oceans

Ocean water covers about 71 percent of Earth's surface. Most of this is in one of five ocean basins (the Pacific, Atlantic, Indian, Southern, and Arctic oceans). All are

▼ The Dead Sea, between Israel and Jordan, is ten times saltier than the world's major oceans. The saltiness makes it easier to float in the Dead Sea than in the oceans.

THE WATER CYCLE

The water cycle restores freshwater supplies in lakes and rivers and creates much of Earth's weather. When water evaporates from oceans and lakes (and from plants), it goes into the lower levels of the atmosphere as water vapor. This may be carried higher by air currents. When the surrounding air is cool enough, the water vapor forms tiny droplets on particles of dust to form clouds. Many droplets may join together to form bigger drops. These fall as rain or snow on the oceans or land. There, the water runs into rivers and soaks into the topsoil.

connected parts of the World Ocean. Ocean currents move cold water from high latitudes to tropical regions, and the other way. The combined area of the World Ocean is 139 million square miles (361 million sq. km). It has a volume of 310 million cubic miles (1.3 billion cubic km) and an average depth of 12,435 feet (3,790 m).

The World Ocean sits largely on oceanic crust made of basalt rock, as do two smaller and separated oceans—the Caspian and Black seas. Other large areas of salt water that do not lie on oceanic crust—for instance, the Aral Sea in Kazakhstan and Uzbekistan—are described as salt lakes. Together, saltwater oceans contain 96.5 percent of the

▶ When chunks of ice break off the great Antarctic ice sheets, they form floating icebergs.

total water on Earth and have an average salinity (saltiness) of 3.5 percent, though this varies greatly.

Groundwater and Ice

About 1.7 percent of the hydrosphere is made up of groundwater in pores and crevices in rocks beneath the continents and oceans. Some is fresh and some is salty water. The frozen ice caps of Antarctica and Greenland, plus glaciers in many parts of the world, make up another 1.7 percent of

▲ A blanket of cloud covers low-lying land. Cloud forms when damp air is cooled as it rises over mountains or passes over cold land.

Earth's water. Global warming threatens to melt some of this ice, adding to the liquid water in the oceans—and so raising the sea level. A small fraction of Earth's water is found in the atmosphere and inside animals and plants.

GENERAL INFORMATION

- The combined mass of water in the hydrosphere is about 1.5×10^{18} tons (1.4×10^{18} tonnes).
- Some of the ice in Antarctica is 1 million years old.
- Frozen water locked up in glaciers flows slowly downhill. The fastest glaciers may travel more than 10 miles (16 km) every year.

WATER

Q What lies under the oceans?

A The sea floor (below) has plains, valleys, mountains, and even volcanoes. Near the shore is the shallow continental shelf. This slopes to the plain, about 13,125 feet (4,000 m) below. On the plain are deep cracks called ocean trenches and raised areas called ridges.

Q How much of Earth is covered by oceans?

A The oceans cover 71 percent of Earth's surface. The continents are actually huge islands in a continuous stretch of water (below). The water flows around the world in a pattern of warm and cold currents.

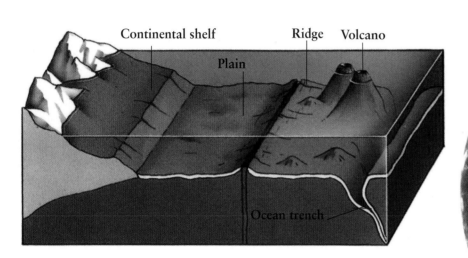

Continental shelf   Ridge   Volcano

Plain

Ocean trench

Q How does the sea change the coastline?

A The waves of the sea constantly pound the edge of the land (right). They change the shape of the coastline in two ways. First, the waves smash against the rocks and grind them into pebbles and sand. They hurl the pebbles at the cliffs, slowly wearing them away. But the sea also moves the sand and pebbles to other places. The coastline is built up where the sea drops them, and beaches are formed.

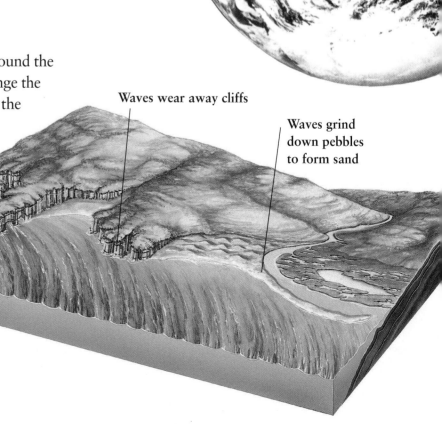

Waves wear away cliffs

Waves grind down pebbles to form sand

Q What is the water cycle?

A Water is always on the move (right), changing from liquid to vapor and back to liquid. The heat of the sun evaporates water from the oceans, lakes, and rivers. Plants also release moisture from their leaves. The moisture rises into the air and cools to form clouds. Winds blow the clouds toward the land. Here, the clouds grow cooler, especially over high ground, and it starts to rain. The rain drains into rivers and lakes and then back into the sea.

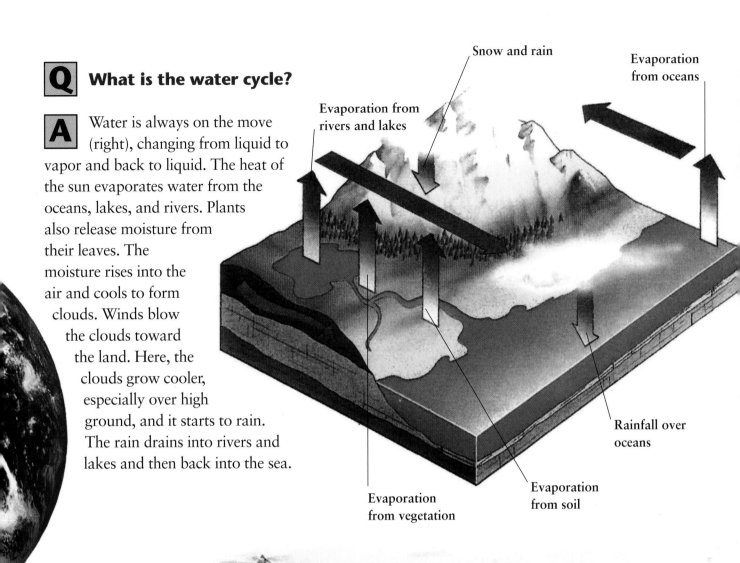

Snow and rain

Evaporation from oceans

Evaporation from rivers and lakes

Rainfall over oceans

Evaporation from soil

Evaporation from vegetation

Q What is a glacier?

A A glacier (right) is a river of ice that forms in cold regions high up in the mountains or near the poles. It slides very slowly downhill, several feet each year. It carries a mass of rocks that scrape away the valley walls and floor. It later deposits rocks and earth in huge ridges called moraines. If a glacier reaches the sea, large pieces break off and float away as icebergs.

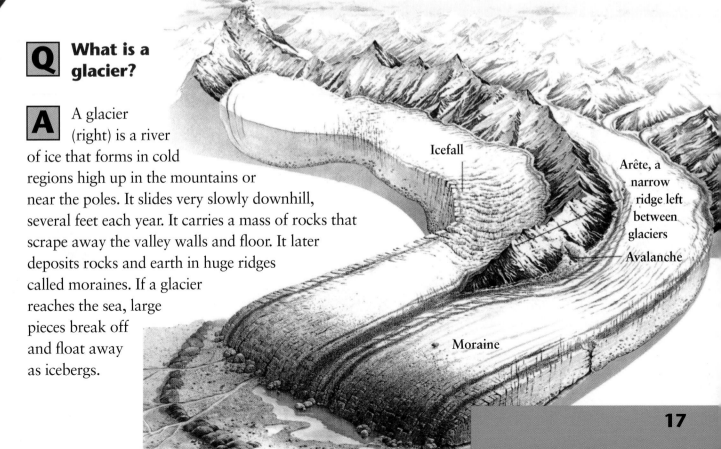

Icefall

Arête, a narrow ridge left between glaciers

Avalanche

Moraine

LANDSCAPE

The natural landscape is a combination of landforms and vegetation. Landscape is the product of many different forces, and they are at work all the time.

KEY FACTS

Highest mountain: Mount Everest, 29,029 feet (8,848 m)

Longest glacier: Lambert Glacier, Antarctica, 250 miles (400 km) long

Longest mountain range: Andes mountains, South America, 4,350 miles (7,000 km)

Some landscapes are relatively new, and others are millions of years old. Many have been altered by the activities of people.

The natural processes that sculpt landscapes are the actions of mountain-building, weather, water, plants, and animals. Over millions of years, Earth's continental crust has been crumpled into mountain ranges and hills.

Any land that is exposed to the atmosphere experiences weathering. This is the gradual breakdown of rocks by freezing, thawing, and chemical processes (for example, the effect of dilute sulfuric acid in raindrops).

▲ Over millions of years, a river has worn its way into these rocky mountains to create a deep gorge.

▼ Small lakes and small, rounded hills cover this landscape in Canada. It is typical of land that was once covered by an enormous sheet of ice.

▲ Ocean waves batter a rocky coastline. Even the hardest rocks are eventually eroded by waves.

▲ Part of this hillside in Thailand has been stripped of its natural forest so that people can grow crops.

FOSSILIZED LANDSCAPES

Earth has warmed since the last ice age, so glaciers and ice sheets are much smaller than they once were. Many landscapes in Canada are dotted with hundreds of small lakes. They were formed when blocks of ice melted and left holes that filled with water—kettle lakes. These are called "fossilized landscapes" because the forces that made them no longer operate.

Weathering weakens rocks and makes it easier for rivers, glaciers, and the wind to erode them (wear them away). Plants sink roots into cracks in the weakened rock. Over time, the cracks widen, topsoil is created, and more plants—grasses, bushes, and trees—grow.

Water and Ice

Over millions of years, rivers and glaciers have carved valleys and carried huge quantities of rock fragments (sediment) to the sea or to lakes, where the sediment is deposited (dropped). Rivers meander, widening their valleys and laying down shingle, sand, or mud.

At the coast, waves batter and erode shorelines. Rubble from eroded cliffs is carried away by ocean currents, broken into smaller fragments, rounded into pebbles, and eventually broken into grains of sand. These are deposited on beaches and sandbars.

Volcanoes and Wind

Volcanoes spew millions of tons of lava and dust onto the land around them, changing the landscape. Earthquakes thrust chunks of land higher. In some regions, the wind blasts grains of sand at rocks, eroding them into weird shapes.

People change landscapes continuously in many ways: by clearing forests for agriculture, reclaiming parts of lakes, altering the course of rivers, building cities, and irrigating deserts.

GENERAL INFORMATION

● Some landscapes have many different types of plants growing on them, while others have few. Much of Siberia is covered by just two species—larch and pine trees.

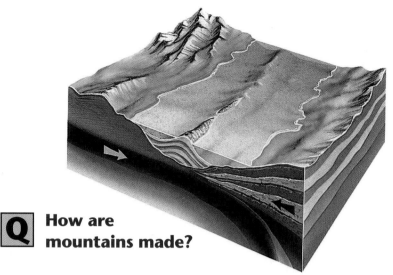

Q How are mountains made?

A The surface of Earth consists of a series of huge plates. These move slowly around and sometimes collide with each other (above). When this happens, the edges of the plates are pushed up, and the layers of rock crumple and fold. Over millions of years, the folds form chains of mountains.

Q How are caves formed?

A Many caves are found in limestone rock (below). They are formed when rainwater soaks down through cracks in the rock. The water dissolves the limestone, making the cracks bigger. Now streams can flow in, underground. They wear away weak parts of the rock to make caves. Sometimes water drips into the caves. The dissolved limestone forms hanging spikes called stalactites. Pillars called stalagmites form on the floor below.

Q What is soil made from?

A Soil is a mixture of rock particles and humus, which is made from the tissues of dead plants and animals. The humus breaks down and releases minerals that help plants to grow. Below the soil is the rocky subsoil, and beneath that is the solid rock known as bedrock.

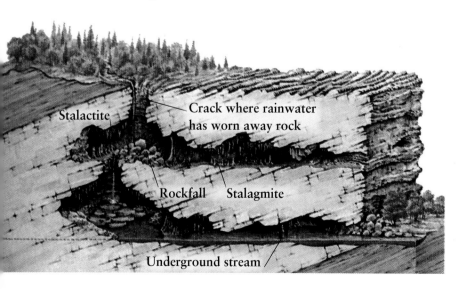

Stalactite

Crack where rainwater has worn away rock

Rockfall Stalagmite

Underground stream

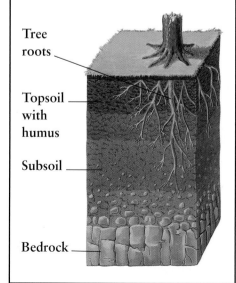

Tree roots

Topsoil with humus

Subsoil

Bedrock

Q How can a river alter the landscape?

A Rivers begin with water flowing downhill (left). Young mountain streams often originate in glaciers. The swiftly flowing water can carve away rock, and it produces deep, V-shaped valleys. As it reaches gentler slopes, it moves more slowly, producing broad valleys. When the river reaches flat plains, it may meander in wide curves. If a curve becomes cut off, it forms a lake. As a river reaches the sea, it deposits stones and sand and may form a delta of low land on the coast.

Q What is an iceberg?

A An iceberg is a piece of ice from a glacier or ice sheet that breaks off at the coastline and then floats in the sea. Only one-eighth of an iceberg shows above the water. This is why they are dangerous to ships. Icebergs may drift for years before they melt.

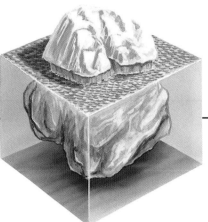

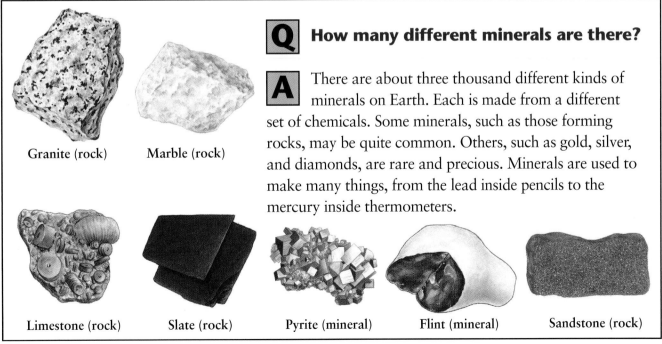

Granite (rock)   Marble (rock)

Q How many different minerals are there?

A There are about three thousand different kinds of minerals on Earth. Each is made from a different set of chemicals. Some minerals, such as those forming rocks, may be quite common. Others, such as gold, silver, and diamonds, are rare and precious. Minerals are used to make many things, from the lead inside pencils to the mercury inside thermometers.

Limestone (rock)   Slate (rock)   Pyrite (mineral)   Flint (mineral)   Sandstone (rock)

ENVIRONMENT

The environment of a place is all its characteristics, including the chemical makeup of the soil, the climate, and the animals and plants—if any—that live there.

KEY FACTS

Hottest environments known to support life: Hot springs and hydrothermal vents with temperatures of up to 285°F (140°C) support simple organisms called hyperthermophiles

Coldest environments known to support life: Polar ice in the Arctic and Antarctic with temperatures as cold as 5°F (–15°C) supports simple life forms called cryophiles

▲ Protea flowers in a South African environment called fynbos; it has over nine thousand plant species.

Every place on Earth has its own physical environment. Terrestrial environments are those on land. They include wet tropical rain forests, open grasslands, and arid, sun-baked deserts. There are also aquatic, or freshwater (rivers, lakes, and swamps), atmospheric, and marine environments.

Marine environments are those found in the ocean. They include the intertidal zone, which is the area from which the sea retreats at low tide. The ocean floor thousands of feet below the surface is another type of marine environment.

▲ Rain forests are home to more than half of Earth's species of animals and plants.

Biotic or Abiotic?

The elements that make one environment different from any other environment can be divided into biotic and abiotic factors. The biotic factors are the animals and plants that live there.

The abiotic elements include climatic factors. Examples are the amount and strength of sunlight, the range of temperature and humidity, the frequency of strong winds, and the frequency and amount of rainfall and fog. Abiotic elements also include the chemical composition of the air, soil, and water—including pollution. Pollution includes the chemicals released into the air when fossil fuels are burned and oil that leaks into the ocean from supertankers.

Species Richness

Different environments suit different forms of life. Some environments have a very limited range of organisms: the icy Antarctic desert, for instance. On the other hand, tropical rain forests, coral reefs, and the fynbos environment of South Africa have thousands of species. The fynbos has varied plant life because its moist, mild winters and hot, dry summers are ideal for different types of plants to flourish.

▲ Organisms that live between the levels of high tide and low tide must be able to live in both salt water and air.

HARSH ENVIRONMENTS

Some environments are very extreme. For instance, hydrothermal vents on the ocean floor spew out very hot water. These vents support invertebrate animals called Pompeii worms, which live in water as hot as 176°F (80°C). The worms have a coating of heat-tolerant bacteria.

▼ An extreme environment: a jet of steam called a geyser.

GENERAL INFORMATION

● Biodiversity is a measure of how many different species live in an environment. Tropical coral reefs and rain forests are the most biodiverse environments.

● An environment may or may not support life. The red-hot lava of a volcano supports no life at all.

Q What causes the winds?

A Winds are created because of differences in air temperature and air pressure. When air is heated at the equator (below), it rises, cools, and then sinks over the tropics. Some air moves back again toward the equator, creating the trade winds. The rest is drawn toward the poles as westerly winds.

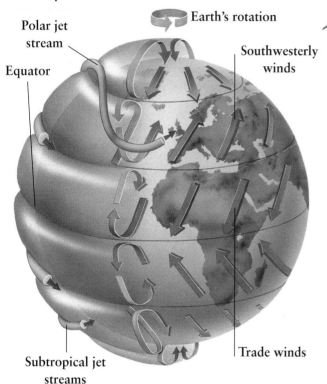

Polar jet stream

Earth's rotation

Equator

Southwesterly winds

Subtropical jet streams

Trade winds

Water vapor in clouds

Water falls as rain

Q How are clouds formed?

A Water evaporates from land, lakes, and sea (above) and is carried by the air as water vapor. Warm air can hold more water vapor than cold air. As warm air rises and cools—for instance, over a mountain—the water vapor condenses to water, forming clouds. Eventually, the water falls from the clouds as rain. The rainwater runs back into the rivers and lakes.

Q What is erosion?

A Erosion is the breaking down of solid rock into smaller particles that are then carried away. Wind, water, gravity, sea, and rain are common natural causes of erosion and so is ice (left). The frozen ice in the glacier carves U-shaped valleys as it moves slowly downhill. Most mountain valleys are formed in this way. Today, human activity also causes damaging erosion.

Ice

Water

Gravity

Wind

Sea

Q What is energy conservation?

A We use a lot of energy in our homes. Much of it comes from oil, coal, or gas, which are fossil fuels that will one day be used up. If we insulate our houses better and trap the sun's heat, we use less fuel. This is called energy conservation. We can also use everlasting energy sources, such as wind.

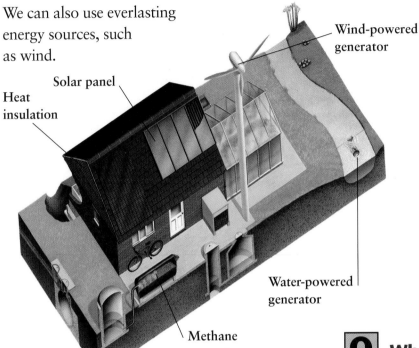

Wind-powered generator

Solar panel

Heat insulation

Water-powered generator

Methane generator

Q Why is pollution harmful?

A Many of the fumes and chemicals produced by cars or industry (below) can damage plants and animals. Even small amounts of some polluting gases or liquids can kill large numbers of living things, and many are poisonous to people as well.

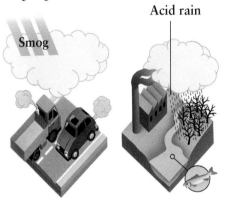

Smog

Acid rain

Q How does the peppered moth adapt to pollution?

A The peppered moth rests on tree bark where its camouflage hides it from bird predators. The bark in polluted towns may be black, and normal camouflage would be useless. In these areas, a black-winged form of the moth is found.

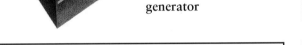

Normal form   Black-winged form

Q What is deforestation?

A Forests once covered fifteen billion acres (six billion ha) of Earth, but now only ten billion acres (four billion ha) are left (below). The process of cutting down trees is called deforestation and is carried out by people. Trees are important to our survival: Like other green plants, they produce oxygen. Without oxygen, animals, including humans, cannot survive.

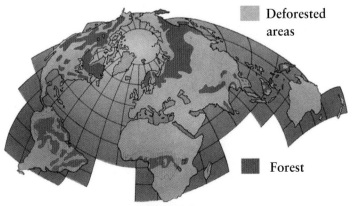

Deforested areas

Forest

HABITATS

A habitat is the set of environmental factors that best suits a species. The best habitat for a wolf is not the same as that for a lion, a shark, a hummingbird, or an oak tree.

▼ Zebras live in tropical grassland habitats. They would not survive in rain forest or dry deserts.

Every species of plant and animal has slightly different needs from its surroundings. That set of features is called the species' habitat.

Plants

Most plants need a supply of nutrients and water, sufficient sunlight for photosynthesis, and support for their roots. However, every plant species has slightly different needs. Some require more moisture; some less. Some can only grow in acidic conditions; others in alkaline soil. Some plants need more sunlight; others less. And many plants depend on certain animals to fertilize them. Therefore, there are thousands of different types of plant habitat.

▲ This bromeliad plant, growing on a tree, has a specialist habitat.

Animals

All animals need food and shelter and suitable places to lay eggs or give birth to young. But they all have different habitat requirements. Some graze on grass, others browse canopy leaves, and yet more hunt other animals.

Some animals need different habitats at different stages of their life. For example, young frogs (tadpoles) and young dragonflies (larvae) have to live in water. Adult frogs can live in water and on land, while adult dragonflies cannot survive in water.

Generalist or Specialist

Some animals and plants are not fussy about where they live. Brown rats can thrive anywhere near buildings and human waste, even in the middle of cities. They are called generalist animals.

Other animals have very particular habitat needs. They are called specialists. Giant pandas need lots of bamboo plants, since this is almost the only thing they eat. In the wild, pandas live in a small part of Tibet and Southwest China. There are not many giant pandas left in the wild.

Habitat Destruction

When a habitat changes a lot, the animals that once lived there may have to move. This may happen if

▼ Giant pandas have specialist habitat requirements.

NICHES

Sometimes two or more types of animals share the same habitat. The curlew (the brown bird, right) and the oystercatcher (the black-and-white bird) are feeding on the same patch of mud. But these two birds have different niches. That means they eat different things in the same habitat. A curlew has a longer beak, so it can grab food that is buried deep in the mud.

a storm blows down the trees in a forest, though the trees will probably grow again after a few years. If people change the habitat by building a city on it, it will never go back to how it once was. This is called habitat destruction. Sometimes it means some species of animals or plants become very rare—or die out completely.

GENERAL INFORMATION

● The habitat of an animal or plant is often made up of several different environments. Not all environments support life, though.

Beaver's lodge

Q What is succession?

A Succession is the natural process by which habitats change, and one community of plants and animals is slowly replaced by another. The picture below shows an example of succession at work, as a temperate lake silts up, and the dry land eventually becomes oak woodland.

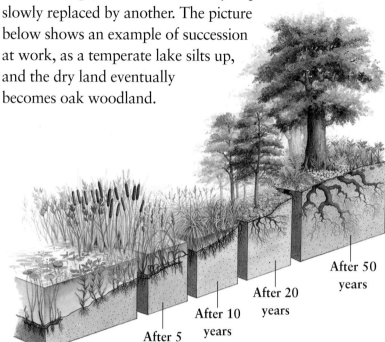

After 5 years

After 10 years

After 20 years

After 50 years

Q Can animals alter a habitat?

A Some animals can change their habitats. For instance, beavers cut down trees with their strong teeth. Then they use the trees, together with mud and stones, to dam streams. Their homes, called lodges, are large piles of sticks built up from the bottom of the ponds they have created (above). Here, they raise their young, safely away from predators.

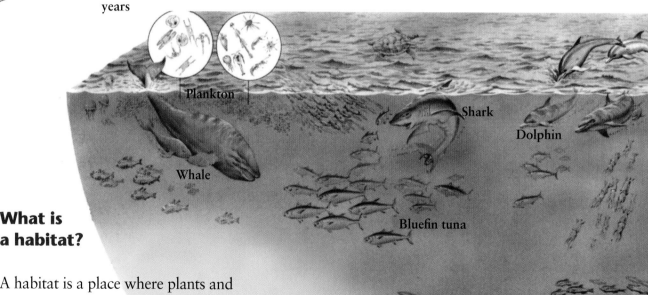

Plankton

Shark

Dolphin

Whale

Bluefin tuna

Giant squid

Deep-sea jellyfish

Anglerfish

Q What is a habitat?

A A habitat is a place where plants and animals live together as a community. Most creatures live in only one type of habitat and cannot survive elsewhere. Look at the different habitats (right) in an ocean. Most life is found near the surface. A few species of fish and squid live in deeper water. The seabed is the realm of specially adapted marine creatures that cannot survive elsewhere in the ocean.

Q What are the world's main land habitats?

A The world's land habitats range from cold tundra and mountains, through hot deserts and grasslands, to the temperate woods and tropical rain forests, teeming with life. The ten major habitats are shown below. Each has its own type of climate, as well as plant and animal life.

Q How do wading birds avoid competing for food?

A These wading birds all have specially shaped beaks for catching different creatures on the seashore. So they do not compete for food, although they live in the same habitat.

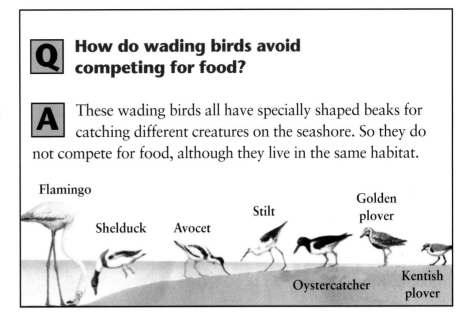

Flamingo

Shelduck

Avocet

Stilt

Golden plover

Oystercatcher

Kentish plover

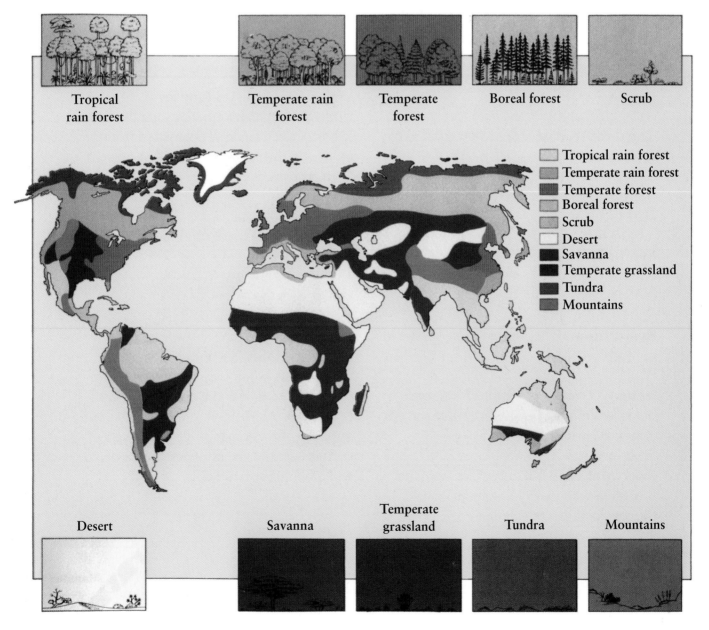

Tropical rain forest

Temperate rain forest

Temperate forest

Boreal forest

Scrub

Tropical rain forest
Temperate rain forest
Temperate forest
Boreal forest
Scrub
Desert
Savanna
Temperate grassland
Tundra
Mountains

Desert

Savanna

Temperate grassland

Tundra

Mountains

GLOSSARY

abiotic Something that is not related to living organisms, such as the weather, in a particular environment.

biodiversity The variety of life on a planet or in a habitat.

biotic Something that is related to living things, such as animals, in an environment.

deforestation The cutting down of trees in a forest, which has a devastating effect on the local wildlife.

erosion The wearing away of land by water or wind.

grassland A large area of land covered by grass; grazing land.

habitat The natural environment where an animal or plant lives.

hydrosphere All of the forms and bodies of water found on or near Earth's surface, including clouds and vapor.

hydrothermal Relating to heated water in the Earth's crust.

iceberg A floating mass of ice that has detached from a glacier or ice sheet and has drifted away in the sea.

intertidal zone An area of seashore that is covered with water at high tide and is uncovered at low tide.

jet stream A thin band of strong, fast wind, several miles above Earth's surface; it normally flows west to east.

latitude The distance of a place north or south of the Earth's equator, measured in degrees.

magma Hot, liquid matter that comes from below the Earth's surface. When it reaches the surface, as in a volcano, it is called lava.

savanna A grassy plain in a tropical or subtropical area, with few trees.

stalactites and stalagmites Underground rock formations that look like icicles. Stalactites grow downward from ceilings in caves; stalagmites grow upward from cave floors.

succession When a community of plants or animals gives way to another until the community becomes stable.

sulfur dioxide A smelly, poisonous gas formed by burning sulfur in air.

tectonic plates Sections of Earth's crust, which, when they move, may cause continents to drift and volcanic eruptions.

volcano A mountain or hill with a vent through which lava, ash, rock fragments, and gases are spewed out.

FURTHER READING

Books

Braasch, Gary, and Lynne Cherry. *How We Know What We Know About Our Changing Climate: Scientists and Kids Explore Global Warming.* Nevada City, CA: Dawn Publications, 2008.

Denecke, Edward J. *First Earth Encyclopedia.* Hauppauge, NY: Barron's Educational Publishing, 2011.

DK Publishing. *First Earth Encyclopedia.* DK First Reference. New York: DK Publishing, 2010.

Heinrichs Gray, Susan. *Geology: The Study of Rocks.* True Books: Earth Science. New York: Scholastic, 2012.

National Geographic Kids. *Planet Earth Collection.* Readers That Grow With You. Washington, DC: 2014

Websites

National Geographic Earth Science
science.nationalgeographic.com/science/earth
Learn all about caves, canyons, and coastlines; erosion and tectonic plates; Earth's atmosphere and deep inside its core. Packed with photos of spectacular caves, amazing minerals, and majestic mountains.

Smithsonian Natural Museum of History: Dynamic Earth
www.mnh.si.edu/earth/text/index.html
Explore this fascinating interactive online exhibit and discover facts about Planet Earth, from tectonic plates, rocks, and mining, to gems, minerals, and more.

World Wildlife Fund
www.worldwildlife.org
Find out about amazing animals from around the world, and learn about their habitats, from this global conservation organization. Discover which species are endangered and what is being done to protect them and their habitats.

Publisher's note to educators and parents: Our editors have carefully reviewed these websites to ensure that they are suitable for students. Many websites change frequently, however, and we cannot guarantee that a site's future contents will continue to meet our high standards of quality and educational value. Be advised that students should be closely supervised whenever they access the Internet.

INDEX